Made in United States
Orlando, FL
31 July 2024

49780123R00057